The Salon Magazine

Ladies and Gentlemen!
Dear Friends!

After 10 issues I have to say THANK YOU VERY MUCH **to Theresa Holstege. Her new and young design made the 2nd** season **of** SALON **looking more contemporary. Now is the time for a change and I am very happy to** WELCOME **Julia Majewski who has agreed to be responsible for the look of the next 10 issues. In the issues of the 1st** season **(1977–1982) there was a list titled:** SALON **is interested in the work of...** followed by the names of artists I admired in these days. Now there is a new list in each issue with the names of musicians, writers and actors and some artists who I admire at the moment (sometimes since many years): Alice in Chains, Amnesia Scanner, Barbara Morgenstern, The Bats, Ben Harper, Black Lung, The Breeders, Courtney Barnett, Kieran Read, Jonah Lomu, Handré Pollard, Faf De Klerk, Aaron Smith, Beauden Barrett, Waisake Naholo, Manu Tuilagi, Andrew Sheridan, Maku Vonipula, Nigel Owens, J.J.Voskuil, Samuel Pepys, Gerbrand Bakker, Bob Odenkirk, Jonathan Banks, Rhea Seehorn, Steve Buscemi, Stephen Graham, Michael K. Williams, Patricia Arquette ...
to be continued!
Should you have any questions, please feel free to contact me at any time.
Best regards,
Gerhard Theewen Editor

Salon is a magazine with original contributions by contemporary artists made especially for the magazine. If not stated the date of the contribution is the year of publishing.
Should, despite our intensive research rights have been overlooked, legitimate claims shall be compensated within the usual provisions.
Subscriptions renew for another year (3 issues) if not cancelled by mail, letter or postcard 3 months before the end of the year.
For information on past issues, see our website www.salon-verlag.de or ask mail@salon-verlag.de

distribution
Buchhandlung Walther König Ehrenstr. 4 D-50672 Köln Tel. +49 (0) 221 / 20 59 653 verlag@buchhandlung-walther-koenig.de

imprint
© 2019 by the contributing artists and Salon Verlag.
editor
Gerhard Theewen
design
Julia Majewski, Köln affairen-gestaltung.de
coverimage
Peter Piller
printing & binding
Online-Druck GmbH & Co. KG
portrait Gerhard Theewen »**Sleepin' on the job**« by **Theresa Holstege**
isbn
978-3-89770-515-9

Bibliographic information published by the Deutsche Nationalbibliothek **The Deutsche Nationalbibliothek lists this publication in the Deutsche Nationalbibliografie;** detailed bibliographic data are available on the Internet at www.dnb.dnb.de.

at

the

moment
(sometimes

since

many

years)

»untitled, 2018«
by Marcel van Eeden

as a gift!

c-print
(20 × 14 cm)

subscribe.

subscribe:

the first **100** **subscribers will get this**

edition of 100, signed and numbered.

mail@salon-verlag.de
For subscription orders please send an e-mail.

Salon

Berresheim
Tim

**Le
Monde
de
Réve
–

Somnambulisme
(Still Grotesque)
I–IV Kopie**

**Dzama
Marcel**

**Marcel's
Movies
of
Maurices
Masks**

Frei
Moritz

**Warten
auf
Godard**

**Frohnapfel
Doris**

Passage

**Gaida
Klaus
G.**

descriptio

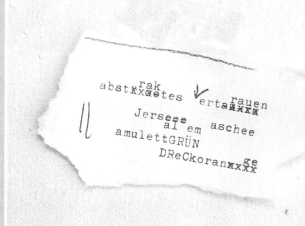

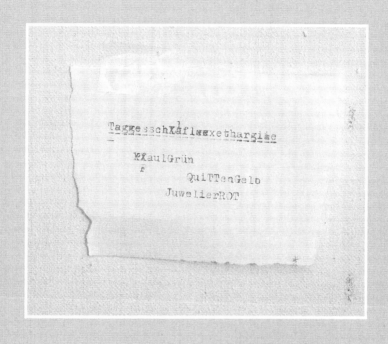

TaggesschXaflmxethargiae
MXaulGrün
QuiTTenGelb
JuwelierROT

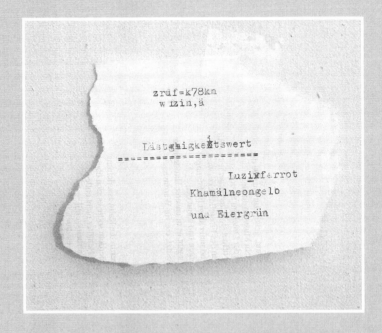

Das Ende der Leinwand

Karfunkel + Modergrün
Horizontblau

**Hantmann
Tobias**

imprints

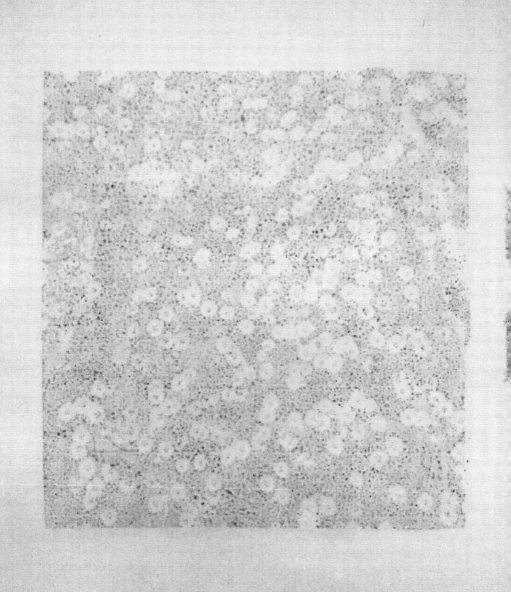

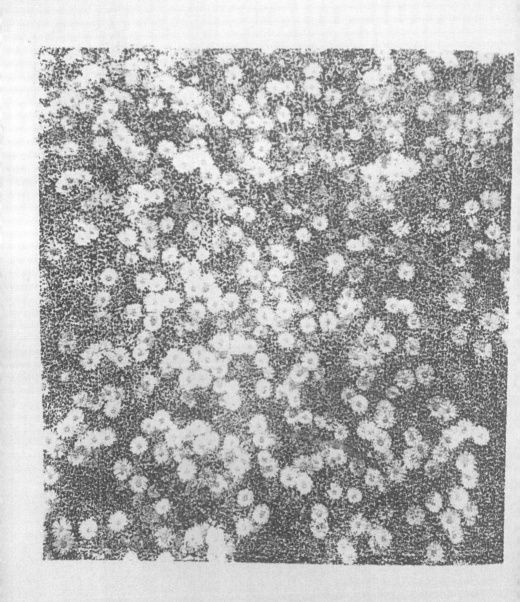

Kocheisen
&
Hullmann

**Zwischenblüte
ambitionierter
Metamorphosen**

**Kuball
Mischa**

**five
suns
–
after
Galileo
TV**

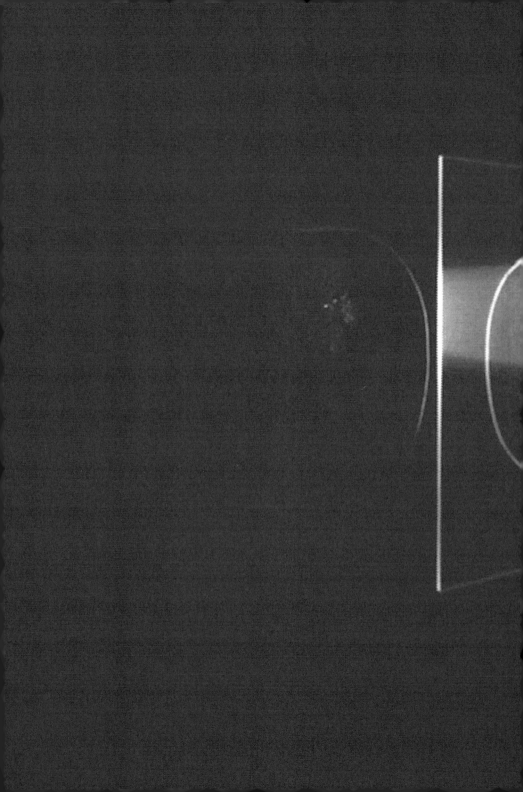

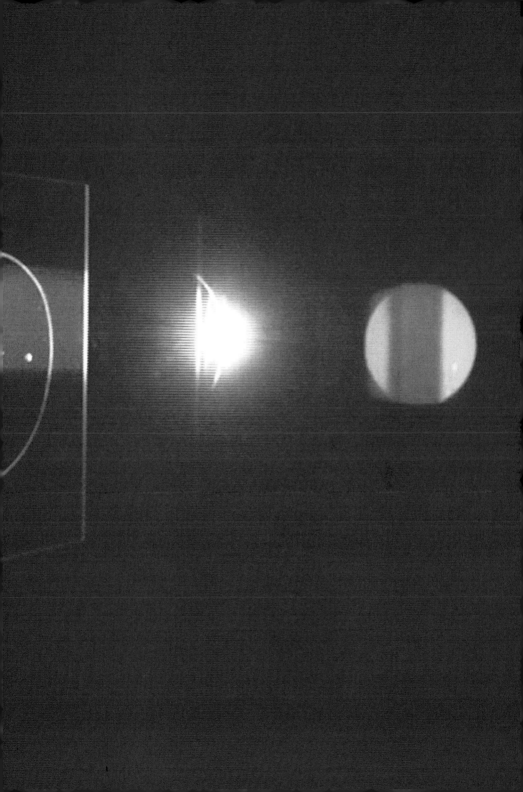

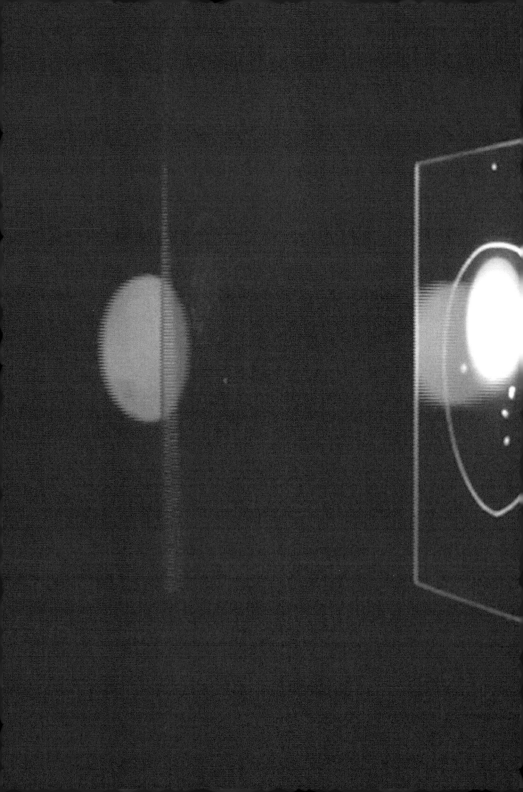

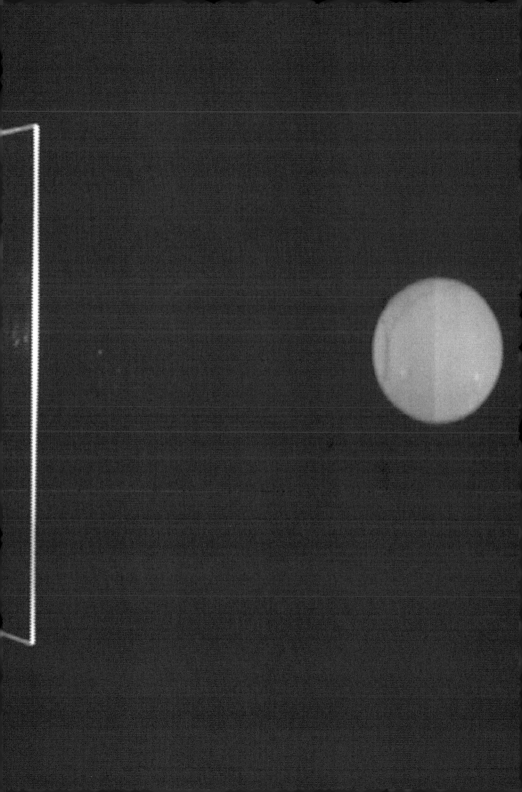

Müller
Josef
Felix

Opa

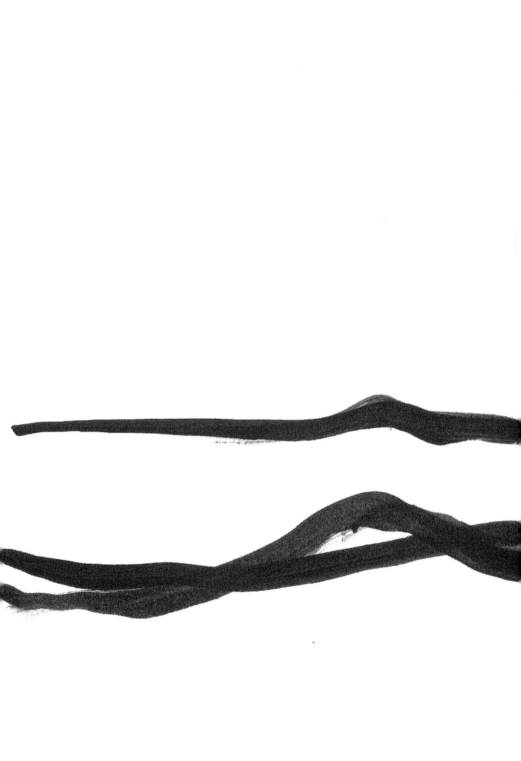

**Müller
Thomas**

vis-à-vis

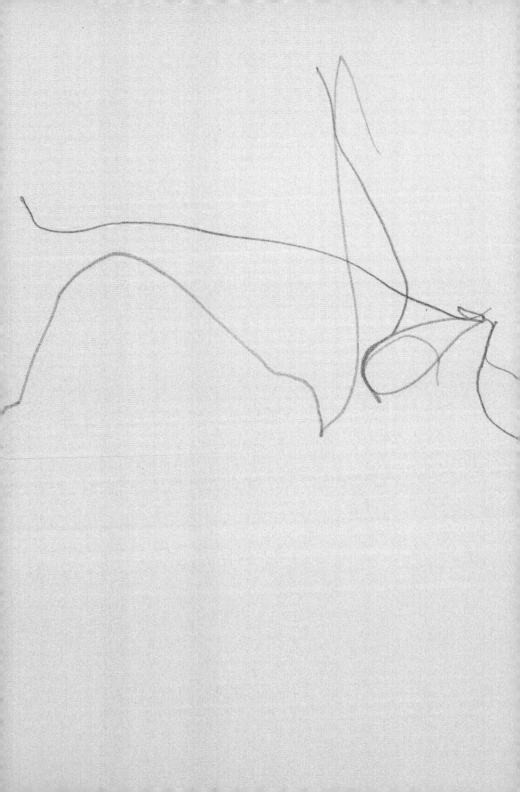

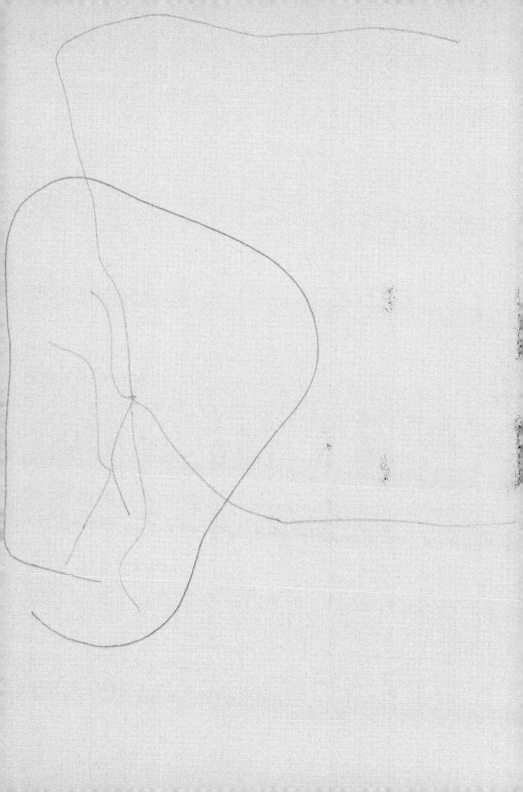

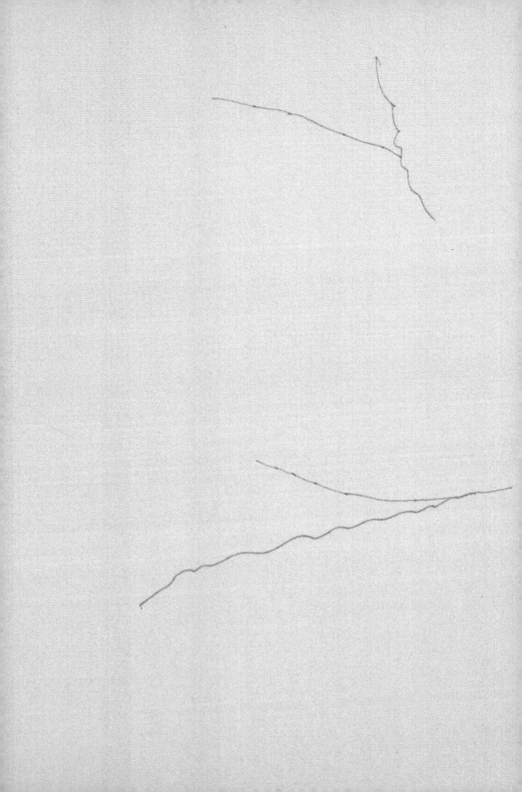

**Rieve
Patrick**

xXx

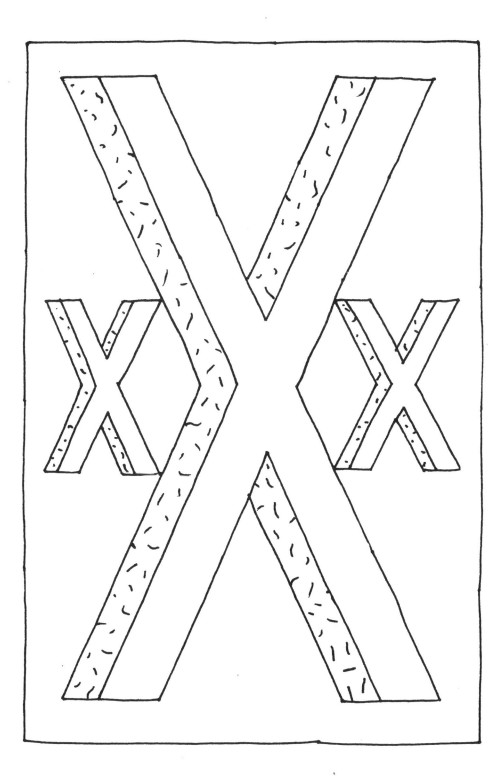

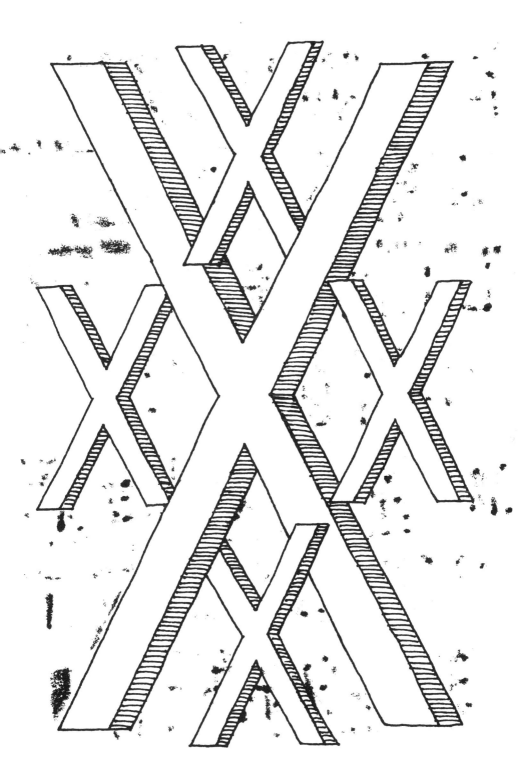

HEY! WE GOT THAT **P.M.A.** WE GOT THAT P.M.A.

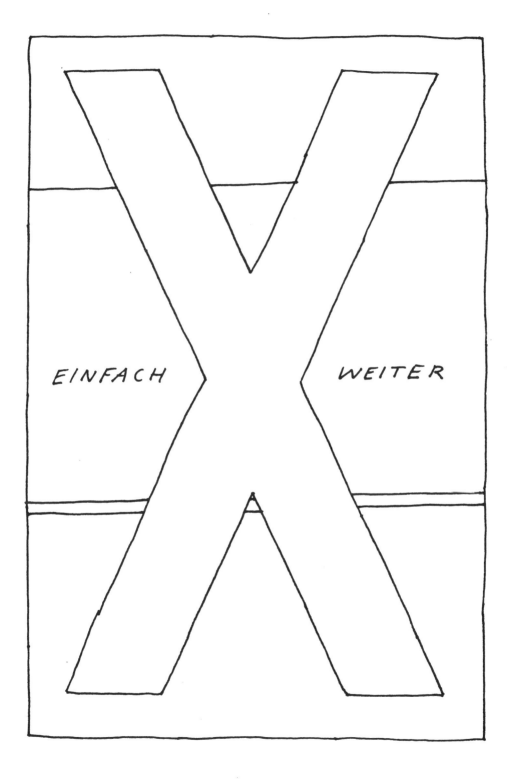

P.R. SAVED THIS TO POSITIVE AND UPLIFTING.

**Uematsu
Keiji**

**Floating
Stone**

Sphinx   BC 2500

The Rock garden, Ryoanji Temple, Kyoto 1500

Osterreische Nationalbibliothek, Wien 1723~1726

Die Freiheitsstature, Paris 1885

Montparnass. Paris 1895

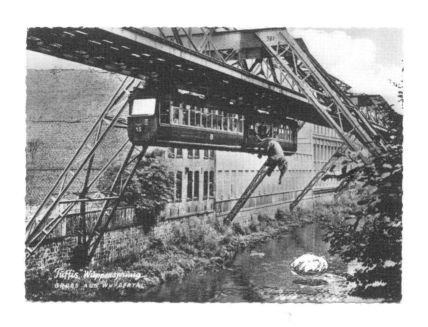

"Tuffis" Wuppersprung aus der Schwebebahn 1950

Blick vom Alter Markt auf dem Dom 1945

Earthrise   Dec.24.1968 Apollo 8

added

carte blanche

SALON VERLAG

out now & coming soon!

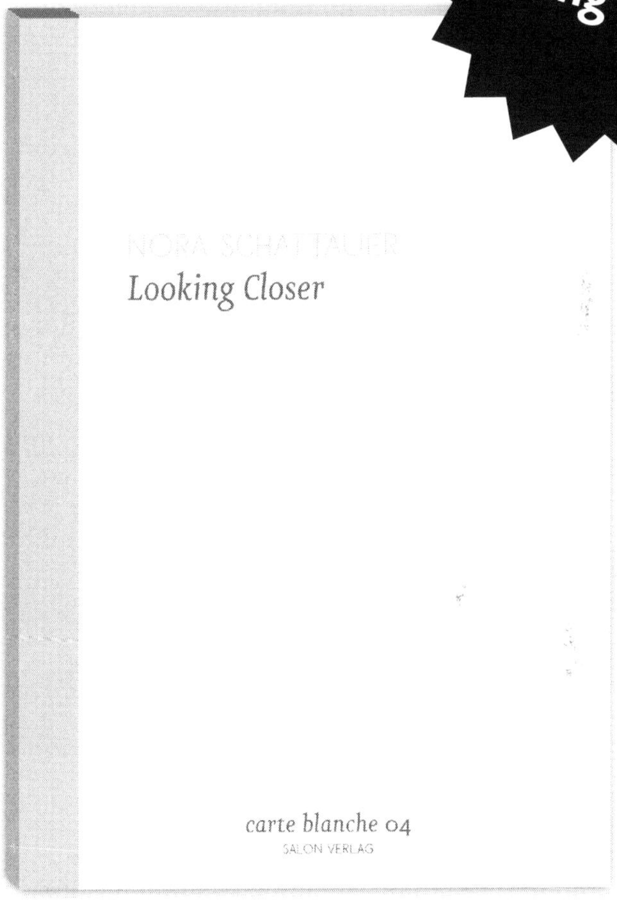

NORA SCHATTAUER
Looking Closer

carte blanche 04
SALON VERLAG

THE NEW ARTIST'S BOOK SERIES.
EDITED BY GERHARD THEEWEN

01 MARCEL VAN EEDEN **ISBN 978-3-89770-483-1** **02** MARK DION **ISBN 978-3-89770-482-4**
03 MARCEL DZAMA **ISBN 978-3-89770-483-1** Preview **04** NORA SCHATTAUER **ISBN 978-3-89770-484-8**
05 CHRIS NEWMAN **ISBN 978-3-89770-485-5** **06** FRANZ ERHARD WALTHER **ISBN 978-3-89770-486-2**

For collectors editions send an email to: mail@salon-verlag.de / Copies of the books can be ordered at eva.moeller@buchhandlung-walther-koenig.de

FLUXPOST
Horst Tress

ART FOR ALL · Fluxpostphoto Horst Tress

MAIL ART IS ROCK 'N' ROLL
HORST TRESS

MAIL ART IS ROCK 'N' ROLL
HORST TRESS

KUNST IST NERVENSACHE
Horst Tress

KUNST IST NERVENSACHE
Horst Tress

https://fluxpost.jimdo.com/

kolle_kuntz

Atelier Showroom Store
Severinstr 128   50678 Köln
www.kolle-kuntz.de   +49 221 34664020

once

upon

a

time
1969

January 13, 1969: Jimi Hendrix Experience in Cologne

February 28, 1969:

Walther König opens his first bookshop in Cologne

July 21, 1969: Neil Armstrong's first steps on the moon

**+ EDITION
VINTAGE**

**+ PARTNER
MARTIN BOHN**

köln

formformsuche.de

THE NEW ARTIST'S BOOK SERIES.
EDITED BY GERHARD THEEWEN.

01 MARCEL VAN EEDEN ISBN 978-3-89770-483-1 **02** MARK DION ISBN 978-3-89770-482-4
03 MARCEL DZAMA ISBN 978-3-89770-483-1 Preview **04** NORA SCHATTAUER ISBN 978-3-89770-484-8
05 CHRIS NEWMAN ISBN 978-3-89770-485-5 **06** FRANZ ERHARD WALTHER ISBN 978-3-89770-486-2
For collectors editions send an email to: mail@salon-verlag.de / Copies of the books can be ordered at eva.moeller@buchhandlung-walther-koenig.de

In Memoriam Jørgen Dobloug

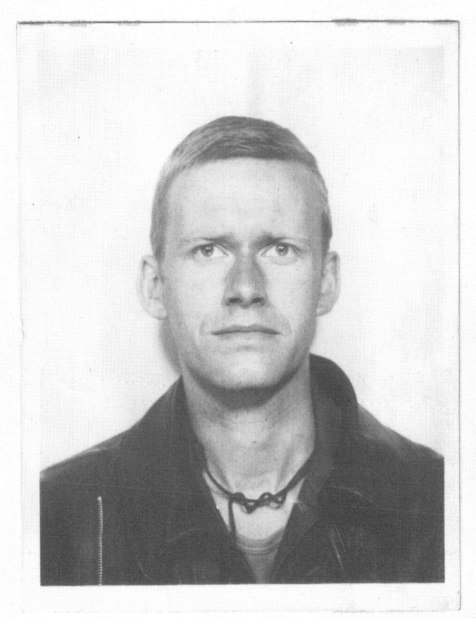

* 23.04.1945 (Oslo)
† 16.01.2018 (Oslo)